Peachtree

A Smart Kid's Q & A Guide

Jeanne Kiefer

Illustrations by Carol Nicklaus

The Millbrook Press   Brookfield, Connecticut

Published by
The Millbrook Press, Inc.
2 Old New Milford Road,
Brookfield, Connecticut 06804

Library of Congress Cataloging-in-Publication Data

Kiefer, Jeanne.
Jobs for kids : a smart kid's Q&A guide / Jeanne Kiefer;
illustrations by Carol Nicklaus.
    p. cm.
Includes index.
Summary: Answers questions about the five most
popular jobs for young people, as well as about other
ways they can make money, with advice on the planning
and marketing involved.
ISBN 0-7613-2611-1 (lib. bdg.)
1. Money-making projects for children—Juvenile literature.
2. Entrepreneurship—Juvenile literature. 3. Success in
business—Juvenile literature. [1. Moneymaking projects—
Miscellanea. 2. Entrepreneurship—Miscellanea. 3. Questions
and answers.] I. Nicklaus, Carol, ill. II. Title.
HF5392.K54 2003   650.1'2'083—dc21   2002008353

Preface

"I want to make some money."

Is that what you were thinking when you picked up this book? If you've already tried working, you're probably looking for new ideas on how to be more successful. If you haven't had a job before, here's a news flash—making money isn't as easy as it looks.

How do I know that? I've talked to hundreds of kids about money. How to spend it, how to save it—and especially how to make it. As editor of a kids' magazine, I spent fifteen years hearing firsthand about lemonade stands that lost money, the world's worst baby-sitting experiences, lawn-mowing jobs from hell, and many other job disappointments. Even successful kids often said that it took a lot of work to make a little cash.

But it doesn't have to be that way. This book is bursting with good ideas on how smart kids can make money and have fun doing it. You'll learn creative ways to advertise, how to set fair fees, what to say to customers, and how to have a business that is both fun and profitable.

Meanwhile, remember that the very best job is one you'd gladly do for free. I'm a living example of that. I've had ten different jobs and loved every one (although I admit to enjoying making money along the way). I hope this book helps you get started on a lifetime of fun at work!

Jeanne Kiefer
Cave Creek, Arizona

Contents

Introduction

If you sit down and read this book closely, there are two things we can guarantee:

- You'll learn about jobs that might be fun to do.
- You'll learn how to make your success more likely.

No, we can't guarantee that you'll find the perfect job or that you'll make a lot of money. Why not? Because some things depend on who you are and where you live. For example:

- Are you old enough for these jobs?
- Do you have enough experience to tackle them?
- Are your parents willing to let you work?
- Is your neighborhood safe enough?
- Does your community have regulations about these jobs?
- Are you willing to do everything necessary to be successful?

We also can't promise that the Q&As in this book will cover everything you need to know to do each job listed here. That would take an encyclopedia!

Jobs for Kids does provide some practical information on each job and points you in the right direction. You'll have to do additional research (such as asking your neighbors about pay rates or calling your town hall about local regulations) to find out how a particular job fits into your community.

In addition, you and your parents should sit down and discuss whether you are responsible enough to handle the tasks necessary for a particular kind of work. Some of the jobs listed in this book aren't suitable for most kids aged twelve or under (baby-sitting, dog walking, and lawn care, for example), and others demand a high degree of responsibility (such as vacation services). Rely on your family members to help you pick an appropriate job—one that will be fun for you and will make the best use of your special talents.

Part 1

First Steps

So, you're all set to start baby-sitting. Or is it a car-wash service you have in mind? Are you already counting up the cash you expect to make selling your homemade fudge?

Wait just one minute. There are a few things to think about before you rush off to work. The Q&As in this section cover some basic questions to ask yourself before you come to any decision about the right job for you.

Thinking About Working

I've never had a job before. What's the most important thing about working?

Surprise! It's not how to find customers, setting fair prices, or even becoming an expert at what you do. They're all important, of course—but here's what adults are *really* thinking when they consider hiring you: **Are you responsible enough for this job?** In other words, will you actually do what you promise to do? Not just the first time, but always?

Here are some things that a responsible worker does, whether he or she is mowing lawns, taking care of pets, or doing other kinds of work:

- Shows up on time and stays until the customer is satisfied
- Has the right attitude—cheerful, respectful, and willing
- Comes prepared, such as dressed for the job
- Finds out what the customer wants before starting
- Does more than the customer expects
- Informs a customer immediately when he or she can't make it to work

Okay, what's the second most important thing about working?

Putting safety first. Your parents and customers want you to be safe, above all. They also are concerned about legal responsibility for any mistakes you make or accidents you have. How can you put their minds at ease? Take absolutely no chances—it is always better to be safe than sorry. Here's how:

- Ask your parents to check out customers before you begin working for them.

- Always let your parents know where you are and what you're doing.

- If you feel uneasy about a customer or task, tell your parents.

- Don't hesitate to call a family member or emergency number for help.

- Discuss safety thoroughly with your customer. Ask questions such as:

  How can I be sure all the house alarms are set?

  Where's a safe place to exercise the dog?

  Do any of the kids have allergies I should know about?

  Will you show me how to operate this mower safely?

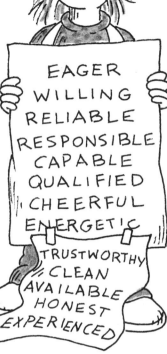

EAGER
WILLING
RELIABLE
RESPONSIBLE
CAPABLE
QUALIFIED
CHEERFUL
ENERGETIC
TRUSTWORTHY
CLEAN
AVAILABLE
HONEST
EXPERIENCED

Thinking About
Jobs

 Q What kind of job is right for me?

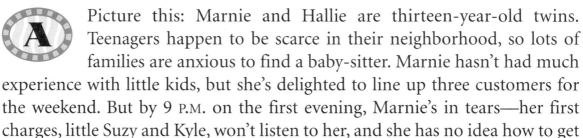 **A** Picture this: Marnie and Hallie are thirteen-year-old twins. Teenagers happen to be scarce in their neighborhood, so lots of families are anxious to find a baby-sitter. Marnie hasn't had much experience with little kids, but she's delighted to line up three customers for the weekend. But by 9 P.M. on the first evening, Marnie's in tears—her first charges, little Suzy and Kyle, won't listen to her, and she has no idea how to get them both bathed and into bed.

On the other hand, Hallie has just one steady customer for her dog-walking service. But she looks forward every day to playing with Snapper and Twinkles, knowing that Mrs. Quincy is always very pleased with her services.

Which twin made the better job choice?

So how do I get started on finding a job that suits me?

 Smart kids spend less time thinking about the money they'll make than about what they'd really *like* to do. If you don't like a job, you probably won't do it for long—no matter how much you are paid. So start by asking yourself a few questions:

- What do I *really* like and what kinds of jobs are related to that? For example:

    Animals—think about jobs like pet walking or watching

    Art—making jewelry or crafts, face painting

    Computers—setup help, calendars, Web development

    Sports—helping the coach, being a practice partner

    Working with kids—baby-sitting, tutoring, helping at a day-care center or with kids' parties

    Working with adults—garage-sale helper

    Gardening—garden helper, growing seedlings, weeding

    Cooking—making jam, cookies, zucchini bread

    Outdoor work—mowing lawns, washing cars

    Other hobbies—magic shows, videotaping, and so on

- Am I old enough and responsible enough for a particular job?
- Do I have enough experience, or do I need to get some? How much do I want to work? A few hours every day? Just now and then?
- Do I want to work alone or with a partner?

The tips in this book will give you some basic information about the jobs mentioned above—but you'll have to sit down with your family to figure out how each one would work in your community. The "My Job Plan" form at the end of this book can help you get started at doing just that.

Thinking About
Job Experience

 Q If I don't already have some experience at a job, how do I learn how to do it?

 A Lots of kids start out by working for no money at all. Their first "job" is volunteering—helping out at their church/synagogue/ library, washing the family car, playing with a toddler while Mom does the laundry, running errands for an elderly neighbor.

Since volunteers aren't paid, there's less pressure about learning to handle the tasks. Before you know it, you've gained some valuable work experience to help you qualify for a paying job.

 Q Is volunteering the only way to learn a job?

 A You probably already know someone who could teach you the basics of the most popular kids' jobs. Maybe your older sister has been baby-sitting for years, or your cousin once had a dog-walking business. Perhaps your father was a master lawn mower as a teenager. Since most people like to give advice, they'll probably be happy to teach you the tricks of the trade.

If you can't dig up an expert coach for a particular job, find out how it is done on your own. If the job is covered in this book, read our tips carefully. If not, search for information on the Internet or at the library. Then practice your skills at home or with a friend before you take on work.

When you're sure you know what you're doing, try to line up just a single paying customer—and ask lots of questions about how the job should be done before you start. Ask for feedback on your work—while you're in the middle of the job and again when it's completed. Make sure customer #1 is happy with your performance before you sign up customer #2.

If you discover that a job isn't right for you, it won't be so disappointing if you haven't already invested a lot of time and energy. You might find that you're too busy with soccer to handle a steady pet-care job or that weekly weeding is just too boring—but that assisting at garage sales is right up your alley.

Every job in this book isn't right for every kid, so don't be discouraged if it takes a few false starts before you find the job that really suits you best.

Thinking About Research

 We're thinking of selling jam from our backyard raspberry patch, but we don't know if anyone will buy it. How can we be sure our idea is a good one?

 Before Sony sells a new video game, the company checks it out with kids to make sure they like it. Before Quaker Oats puts a new cereal on the grocery shelf, it tries to find out if shoppers are likely to snap it up. Businesses do as much research as possible before starting to sell a product or service. You can do this, too, since it means asking just five questions about the job you are considering:

- Who are your customers for this product or service?
  (Who's most likely to buy your jam?)
- Who/what is your competition?
  (Who else is selling homemade jams in your neighborhood?)
- What will attract customers to your product or service?
  (What makes your jam better than a store-bought one?)
- How much will customers pay for this product or service?
  (What is the going price for homemade jam?)
- Where will they buy your product or get the service?
  (Where are they likely to buy homemade jam?)

 I've answered those five questions—now what?

 First, come up with a "marketing plan" based on your research, such as:

- Most of our customers will be women.
- No store in town sells jams like ours (homemade).

- Customers will buy our jam because it is organic, grown and made by local kids, has a pretty label, and is cheaper than other fancy jams.
- They'll pay $3 for a small glass jar.
- They'll buy it from a stand in front of our house.

Now it's time for your creativity to kick in—think of all the ways you can test your plan. In this case, check out fancy jams at the local supermarket, farmer's market, farm stands, and gift shops. Is $3 a reasonable price for a small jar? While checking, examine labels to see how to make your own jars look appealing. How about adding a tag with information on your berry patch?

Then whip up a few samples, attach labels, and show them to a few family friends. Ask for an honest opinion on whether they'd buy the jam and how much they'd pay. Also ask where they might shop for jam like yours, then check out those places.

What if there's something I can't research—like where to set up my stand?

While you won't know whether you've chosen the best location for your stand until you actually set it up, try to gather as much information as possible about other stands. Visit nearby stands and ask yourself: Which ones attract the most buyers, and why? Where do people park? What signs look best? How long are the stands open? How many people stop in an hour? Then put everything you've learned to use. Maybe you'll discover that the most prosperous stands are closer to the corner. This kind of research can help you start off on the right foot in many types of businesses.

You might discover, for example, that you should lower your price. That there's just one other kid (and he's two years younger) selling jams in your neighborhood. Or that pointing out to possible customers that your jam is organic is a good idea.

Thinking About Partners

 My friend wants to be my partner. Chris is a great kid, but is this a good idea?

 Maybe yes, maybe no. Here are some reasons to work alone:

- You don't have to share your earnings and you can make all your own decisions.
- You can work at your own schedule, starting and stopping as you wish.
- You don't risk ruining a friendship if the business goes sour.

Here are some reasons to have a partner:

- It can be more fun to work with a friend.
- You can share tasks (one does it one day, the other the next).
- You can bring more talents to the job (one is an artist, the other a salesperson).
- You can discuss the work and share decisions.
- A team may seem more responsible to adults.
- You can take on more work or bigger jobs.
- It might be safer not to work alone.

 What should I think about when choosing a partner?

 Ask yourself these questions to determine partnership potential:

- Is he always fun to be with, or do you often disagree? Working together means making decisions together, so beware if you often hassle over things.

- Can you really depend on her? If she's sloppy about her homework or forgets her promises, can you really trust her to do her share?

- Can he bring anything special to the business? Maybe he's less shy about talking with adults or has more experience than you do.

- What kind of partnership will she want? Does she just want to be your helper, or will she expect to have an equal say in every decision?

- Does he or she care as much about this partnership as you do? It creates a problem if one person works harder than the other. If partners don't share ideas, you are almost sure to flop as a business—and maybe even as a friendship.

Before taking on a partner, always discuss in full detail what the business will be like and who will do what. Use the "My Job Plan" form at the end of this book to work out your relationship. After all, if planning with your partner isn't fun, what's the chance that the business will succeed?

Part 2

The Five Most Common Jobs

Young people have been doing these five jobs for generations, so these jobs automatically come to mind when we think about kids' jobs. That means you shouldn't have to work too hard to find someone to show you the ropes or to convince adults you can handle them. On the other hand, you might have to work extra hard to beat out the competition from all the other kids in your neighborhood!

Need a Reliable Baby-sitter?

I've had experience with kids
aged 6 months to 8 years.
And I work weekends!

Please call for more information.

Holly, age 12
456–9571

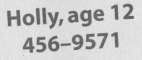

Holly
Baby-sitting
456–9571

Holly
Baby-sitting
456–9571

Holly
Baby-sitting
456–9571

Holly
Baby-sitting
456–9571

Holly
Baby-sitting
456–9571

Holly
Baby-sitting
456–9571

Holly
Baby-sitting
456–9571

Baby-sitting

I want to start baby-sitting Timmy, my neighbor's little boy. But my mom says I'm not old enough. I think I am—how can I change her mind?

Your mother has a point. An experienced sitter will tell you this job can be trickier than it looks. Do you know what to do if Timmy refuses to go to bed? If Janine cries for two hours straight? If Lester cuts his finger, Leah smacks Jamie, or the toilet overflows? What if the dog starts growling at you, the house gets creepy after 10 P.M., or Mrs. Rivas is really late coming home? And is that smoke you smell?

If you honestly believe that you're up to these challenges, then you must prove to your mother and customers that you're fully capable of caring for a child and handling emergencies. If you can't do this, it's best to wait until you are completely ready for the responsibility. Taking care of a child is the most important job you'll ever have.

How can I prove I'm ready for sitting?

A good first step is taking a baby-sitting course. The Red Cross or a local hospital may offer classes on child care and first aid. Having a certificate showing that you've completed such a course can be very helpful in convincing someone to hire you. Then, to get hands-on experience, seek out a situation where you can look after children while being supervised by an adult. For example, offer to be a "mother's helper" to a neighbor, entertaining her toddler while she's doing at-home chores. Or volunteer at your church's day-care center. If you do a good job, these adults might be willing to put in a good word for you.

I just got my first baby-sitting job, watching the Collins twins next week. Any tips for doing the job right?

 Here are a few basics for responsible sitters:

- Meet with the family to get acquainted before the job, if possible.
- Be on time or a little early.
- Write down all contact/emergency numbers, medical conditions, and so on (see the baby-sitting form on page 29).
- Make sure you know exactly what the family wants you to do with the kids.
- Play with the kids and/or read to them so the experience is a good one.
- Don't open the door to strangers or give information over the phone.
- Don't invite friends over, use the phone, or raid the refrigerator without asking permission first.
- Take careful phone messages.
- Leave the house in good order—wash dishes, put away toys, and so on.
- After the job, tell the parents how things went.

 I often baby-sit eight-year-old Nancy, but she can be hard to handle once her parents leave. Can anything make it more fun for both of us?

 Keep naughty Nancy happy with new activities. Experienced baby-sitters put together a goody bag to take along on jobs. It may hold videos, puzzles, books, toys, crafts projects, games—anything that's new and different for the child. How about doing a project together, such as baking cookies or putting on a puppet show? The Internet is a super place to get ideas for keeping kids occupied. Check the sites on page 111, or use your browser to find sites with baby-sitting tips.

Q Last Saturday I baby-sat for four hours, but Mr. Swinton gave me only $8. I didn't think that was enough, but I was too shy to tell him.

A Before accepting your first job, find out the usual hourly fee for a baby-sitter your age by asking your neighbors or other sitters. (Older kids can often charge more.) If customers don't ask you what you charge, let them know the typical neighborhood rate. It's often okay to ask for a bit more if you are caring for more than two kids or taking on extra duties (such as cooking a meal). On the other hand, you might want to offer a special discount to your steady customers.

Q I have one or two baby-sitting customers, but I'd like more. How do I find them?

A Your satisfied customers are your best source for new jobs. Ask them for the phone numbers of friends who might be interested in your services, and then call those families to let them know you are available. You might also tack up a poster at your church or synagogue or community center. Surprisingly, another good source can be your competition—some baby-sitters are really busy (especially on weekends) and may be glad to pass on extra jobs to a responsible backup sitter. This arrangement is good for both of you. Anyone can come down with the flu or have a must-attend soccer game, so it's smart to have another sitter's name to pass on when you can't take a job.

My Baby-sitting Form

Names and ages of children:

Parents' names:	**Address:**	**Phone number:**
Date/time of job:	**Pick-up/drop-off arrangement:**	**Hourly or job rate:** $

EMERGENCY NUMBERS

For parents:	**For neighbor/relative:**	**For poison control:**
For police:	**For fire department:**	**For children's doctor:**

Safety information (emergency exits, fire extinguishers, flashlights, first-aid kit, fuse box, house key):

Medical information (allergies, medical conditions, etc.):

CHILD-CARE INSTRUCTIONS

Bedtime and/or naptime routine:

Food/snacks allowed:

Rules (what's allowed and what is not):

Favorite games:

Other:

LEMONADE

FRESHLY MADE
and
ICY COLD!

We also have
homemade muffins
and oatmeal cookies
YUM YUM YUM YUM

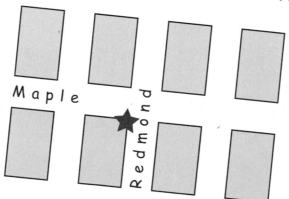

Corner of Maple and Redmond

Lemonade Stand

 My sister and I had a lemonade stand last summer, and it was a total flop. We sat in the hot sun for two hours and only one person stopped. Is it possible to have a stand that makes money?

 When you think about kids' businesses, what pops to mind? First up is a lemonade stand—with happy kids selling icy glasses of delicious lemonade to dozens of eager customers. What's wrong with this picture? As you found out, sometimes the lemonade isn't icy or delicious, the customers aren't buying, and the kids are anything but happy. But it doesn't have to be that way—if you do some advance planning and preparation.

 Where's the best place to have a lemonade stand?

 The answer to that question depends on a second one: Who will be your customers? Mostly hot and thirsty adults, right? Now think about places where lots of sweaty grown-ups gather. If they're strolling past your house in large numbers, you're all set. If not, find another location.

Here are some good sites: next to a biking or running path; near a tennis court, ballfield, park, or playground; at a garage sale or a commuter-route corner with a long stoplight.

Smart Kids Tip

Location

When choosing a spot to set up your stand, make sure it's a safe place and that you have permission to set up there.

When you pick a spot, keep in mind the setup required for a successful stand. There are loads of supplies to truck in and out, and having running water nearby is a plus. Don't ignore the sun situation, either. A shady location will be a blessing for both you and your thirsty customers.

 What's the best time of day to sell lemonade?

 People start thinking "cold drink" when the sun is really hot and high. Setting up for two hours each afternoon may make more sense than sitting out there for a full day.

Q Exactly what do I need to set up a lemonade stand?

A Start with a table—sturdy and large enough to comfortably hold everything. Find a pretty tablecloth big enough to hang down and hide the extra supplies stored underneath the table. Add a few portable chairs for you and your customers. Then gather your supplies. Here are some things you'll need:

- Lemonade concentrate
- Water
- Pitchers and stirrers
- Paper/plastic cups
- Straws
- Napkins
- Money box with lots of change (dollars and coins)
- Cooler with ice and scoop
- Garbage can and plastic liners
- Wagon for hauling supplies
- Sturdy boxes for extra supplies
- Posterboard for additional signs, markers, tape, scissors, thumbtacks

Last of all, create a large sign, listing your prices, to post near your stand.

Q But what if customers don't show up?

A People don't wander around searching for a lemonade stand—you'll have to do something special to attract their attention. Tack a colorful poster with direction arrows or a simple map on all the nearby corners. Then make your stand noticeable with colorful signs, pots of bright flowers, balloons, cheery music from a boom box, or even by wearing a

cute costume. And remember to smile and wave at passersby and offer free samples. Friendly gestures will make your stand much more welcoming.

 What can we sell at our stand? We want to offer more than lemonade.

 Good for you! Lemonade is the old standby, but other items can sell even better. Depending on your customers, you can sell muffins, cookies, brownies, zucchini or banana bread, iced tea or coffee, bottled water, cans of soda, flowers and veggies from your garden, and so on. Store-bought items are easiest to get, but many adults will gladly pay extra for tasty homemade goodies. Just make sure you charge enough to pay for all your supplies and still make a profit. And be sure to find out beforehand if it's all right to sell such things in your town without a license.

 I want to offer something homemade, but I'm not much of a cook. Any suggestions?

 Any basic cookbook has recipes for easy-to-bake brownies or chocolate-chip cookies. If your customers might like a healthier treat, try these muffins. You can make them in mini or regular size.

Oatmeal Muffins
Makes 10 to 12 regular muffins

1. Preheat oven to 400 degrees F.
2. Place paper muffin cups in muffin tins.
3. Combine these dry ingredients in a large bowl:

   1 ½ cups flour

   ¾ cup rolled oats (not instant)

   ½ cup sugar

   2 teaspoons baking powder

   ¼ teaspoon salt
4. Combine these wet ingredients in a small bowl:

   1 beaten egg

   ¾ cup milk

   ¼ cup vegetable oil
5. Gently stir the wet ingredients into the dry, until just moist (batter should be a little lumpy).
6. Spoon the batter into muffin cups, filling each about 2/3 full.
7. Bake until golden—about 20 minutes for regular, 12 minutes for mini.
8. Cool on a wire rack.

We all love the Pet Patrol!

- $2 per 15-minute walk/feeding visit
- $5 per 30-minute play period
- Other services on request
- Discounts for monthly arrangements

Call your pet's best friends today!

Jenny, Cher, and Lauren
555-8333

(Among us we own 6 dogs, 3 cats, 4 gerbils, and a parrot!)

Pet-Care Service

Q My sister Jenny and I just love cats, dogs, snakes, and *all* animals. Is there a job for us?

A Are you really responsible? Have you had lots of experience taking care of your own pets? Do you have plenty of time to spare after school, on weekends, and on holidays? Then think about starting a pet-care business. Some pet owners will gladly pay to have a responsible young adult stop by their houses to walk, feed, or play with their animals. Service can vary widely—from one visit every weekday for busy people to two or three visits a weekend for vacationers.

If you have the proper experience, you could also clean cages and tanks and care for birds, small animals, reptiles, and fish.

I take care of our beagle, Sandy, but Mom says I'm not old enough to pet-sit our neighbor's Doberman. Why is she being so unreasonable?

Sandy is small and friendly and loves you to bits. No wonder it's a snap to feed and walk her. But your mother knows that caring for other people's pets is often another story altogether.

Many dogs can be hard to handle, cats can be nervous, and it's quite common to find a parrot that bites! This job also involves going into empty houses. For those reasons, pet care is a business for older kids (at least twelve) with lots of solid experience with animals.

If you're old enough and believe you can handle the responsibility, ask your mother if you can start out in a small way. Begin by looking after small animals—fish, birds, or hamsters—for one or two days at a time. You might also volunteer to help out at the local pet shelter. Once you prove yourself fully capable, your mother might agree that you can move up to caring for dogs and cats.

Mrs. O'Hara asked me to care for her poodle, Sweetie, for a weekend. What do I need to know?

 Once your parents have said okay, sit down with Mrs. O'Hara to go over all the arrangements.

- Use a form like the one shown on page 43. Don't rush this first session—both of you need to be perfectly clear on what's involved. For example, ask about the time the job begins and ends, payment, exactly what the tasks are, where the food is stored, how many treats are allowed, and so on.

- If Sweetie isn't your best buddy already, play with her and hand out treats, with her master looking on. She'll be happier to see you (and the treats you always have on hand) when you do return to take care of her. Take her for a short walk to see how she behaves on a leash.

- The prejob visit lets you see if you can handle the assignment. Maybe Sweetie isn't quite as sweet as you expected. Or Rags pulls so hard that you have to struggle to hold on to his leash. It's always better to politely turn down a job than to take on more than you can safely handle.

- If you do take the job, Mrs. O'Hara and Sweetie will be depending on you, so you must be extra responsible about your duties. Continue to care for any pet until you're sure the owner has returned home. Sometimes plans change, and the owner isn't able to contact you. Be safe rather than sorry in all that you do.

 When I go over to feed Snuggles, my neighbor's cat, she always hides from me. Am I doing something wrong?

 If her food is eaten and the litter box is used, she's probably just fine. Pets often become anxious and act oddly when their owners are away. It's part of your job to ease their stress. Sometimes that calls for giving Rags (who is bored) an exciting romp in the backyard, and sometimes for just taking a peek into the closet to make sure Muffin (who is shy) is okay. If you think something might really be wrong, ask your parents for advice. If they agree, you can always call Snuggles's owner, who will welcome your concern about her precious pet.

 I know I'd be good at taking care of pets, but why would people hire me?

 What if Mr. Smith saw you walking a dog past his house—and noticed that your T-shirt said "Kerry's Pet-Walking Service, 555-6677"? Or maybe Mrs. Sahib saved the colorful flyer you left dangling from her doorknob (with a little dog biscuit attached). Since pet care usually calls for lots of visits, you'll want to concentrate on customers in your own neighborhood. Luckily, that's also the easiest place to identify the "pet" homes that will be good targets for your advertising. Once you've signed up a few people, ask them if you can use their names as references for future customers. And you're on your way!

Smart Kids Tip

Be a Pet Pal

Always approach a pet slowly, speaking in a soft and soothing voice. Sneaking up on an animal or using fast hand motions can scare it, especially if it's been sleeping.

Let animals eat in peace—many will act to protect their food.

Before walking any dog, check that the collar and leash are secure. Be sure you can control the dog if it tugs hard, such as when spotting a cat. Avoid any area where you might meet unfriendly dogs or other critters.

Carry plastic baggies to pick up dog waste if your community requires it.

Q Two kids in my area are already walking dogs. How can I stand out?

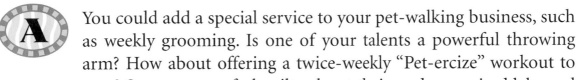 **A** You could add a special service to your pet-walking business, such as weekly grooming. Is one of your talents a powerful throwing arm? How about offering a twice-weekly "Pet-ercize" workout to your customers? Some owners feel guilty about their underexercised labs and spaniels, so a strenuous session with a tennis ball or Frisbee could be a real selling point. Just be sure you have a safe, fenced area for this kind of activity. Another plus could be doing extra chores on daily visits, such as taking in mail and watering plants. You might want to tack a little onto your usual fee for this extra service.

My Pet-Care Form

Names of pets with ID numbers:		
Owner's name:	**Address:**	**Home phone:**
Date/time job starts:	**Date/time job ends:**	**Payment agreement:**

EMERGENCY NUMBERS

For owner:	For neighbor:	For vet:

House information (keys/locks, security system, fuse box or circuit breaker, fire extinguisher, flashlights, first-aid kit, cleaning products, etc.):

Other information (where pet supplies are located, etc.):

PET-CARE INSTRUCTIONS

Feeding/watering instructions (What? How much? How often? Where? When?):

Care instructions (Petting? How long? When? Playing or walking? How long? When? Other?):

Treats? (What? When? How many?):

Cleanup instructions (Litter box? Poop scooping? Other?):

Pet likes, dislikes, fears, habits, behaviors, and medical conditions:

Other:

CAR WASH Early Bírd Specíals

Sign up now for 3 car washes and get up to $2.00 off our everyday low prices!

Car Wash—usually $5, but NOW $4!
Wash, Vacuum, Wax: usually $12, but now $10!
You must sign up by July 31 to get the discount.

Call Sam and Jennifer today!
667-5433

Car-Care Service

 Q My stepdad says I do a super job on our family car. How can I get started making money by washing other people's cars?

 A If you have the skills and the will to work hard to satisfy customers, you're halfway there! Kick off your business plan by deciding which services you'll offer to customers.

Washing only?
Waxing?
Cleaning and vacuuming the interior?
Will you work alone or with a friend?

Washing and waxing can take hours, so sharing the chore with a partner might make it a lot more fun—but you'll also have to share the earnings. Since you'll have to travel to the location of the car with your materials, think about what neighborhoods would be best for finding customers.

 Q Mr. Purdy asked me to clean his car on Saturday morning. Do I have to bring along anything to do this job?

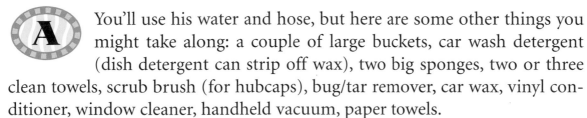 **A** You'll use his water and hose, but here are some other things you might take along: a couple of large buckets, car wash detergent (dish detergent can strip off wax), two big sponges, two or three clean towels, scrub brush (for hubcaps), bug/tar remover, car wax, vinyl conditioner, window cleaner, handheld vacuum, paper towels.

For your first few jobs, your parents might let you use their supplies. If you intend to make this a steady business, however, invest in your own equipment.

I could use some advice on exactly how to wash and wax a car.

 Here are some tips on washing and waxing a car:

- As a general rule, cars should be washed about once or twice a month and waxed twice a year.
- Avoid scratching the paint—use clean sponges and towels, wear clothing without zippers and buttons, and keep the hose pressure at medium.
- Avoid washing or waxing in direct sunlight—ask the owner to park in the shade, or come early or late in the day.
- Start the wash by hosing down the whole car to soften dirt.
- Apply a special cleaner to soften tar and bugs (mostly in front of the car).
- If the car is really dirty, first soap up and rinse off lower parts, then discard the dirty water. Use a soft scrub brush to clean the wheels.
- Now wash the whole car in sections, using a clean, soapy sponge and working from top to bottom, hosing down as you go to keep soap from drying on the car.
- Hose down the car once more and rinse the wheels and under the car.
- Dry the car with clean towels or a sponge cloth.
- Once the car is clean and dry, apply wax according to the instructions on the container.
- When the wax dries to a haze, rub it off with a clean cotton towel, working in sections. Then buff the entire car once again with a soft cloth.
- Apply vinyl conditioner to a sponge or rag and clean vinyl areas such as roof racks and trim.
- Clean the windshield and windows last.

Before you pack up your supplies, ask the customer to go over the car and point out anything that isn't okay. Keep working until he or she is completely satisfied—that's a sure way to keep your customers coming back!

 Q What's the best way to clean the inside of the car?

 A Follow these tips:

- Take out the floor carpets, shake and vacuum well.
- Empty ashtrays and other compartments.
- Vacuum the interior thoroughly, especially all the narrow spaces.
- Use a sponge to wipe interior surfaces (use Endust on a cloth first if the interior is very dusty).
- Apply vinyl conditioner to a sponge or rag and clean vinyl surfaces like the dashboard.
- Clean the windshield and windows last.

47

I have two customers in my neighborhood, but I'd like more. How do I get them?

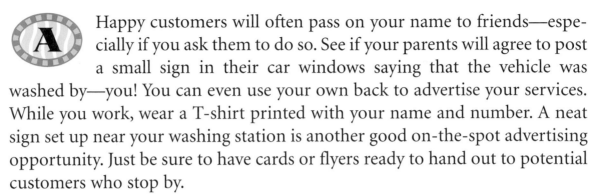 Happy customers will often pass on your name to friends—especially if you ask them to do so. See if your parents will agree to post a small sign in their car windows saying that the vehicle was washed by—you! You can even use your own back to advertise your services. While you work, wear a T-shirt printed with your name and number. A neat sign set up near your washing station is another good on-the-spot advertising opportunity. Just be sure to have cards or flyers ready to hand out to potential customers who stop by.

Speaking of flyers—they're a great way to drum up new business. Drop them off house-to-house or post them (adding tear-off tabs with your name and phone number) on community bulletin boards.

If you want to make a big splash, volunteer to help with a charity car wash for a local cause such as the animal shelter or library. Organizing an event like this is a big deal and is best left to adults, but you can suggest the idea and offer to provide some workers (rounding up friends, relatives, and neighbors to help). Ask for public acknowledgment of your contribution—and take the opportunity to pass out your cards or flyers to those who attend.

 Last month I washed and waxed Mrs. Roberts's car. I see her driving around the neighborhood and her car could really use another wash. But I'm embarrassed to ask her for more work. Should I forget about it?

Asking an adult for work can be hard. It helps to have a sales gimmick to get you started. How does this sound? "Mrs. Roberts, this is Jimmy Berger. Remember, I washed your car last month? I'm calling to let you know that I have a monthly service offering for my customers. It's $1 off per wash if you sign up for three once-a-month washes." Or:

"I'm stopping by to drop off a discount flyer. You'll get $1 off the next two washes." Or: "Would you be interested in a coupon book for $20? It includes three washes and one wax job." The point is to give your customers a good reason to call you. Just about everyone likes a bargain, so this sort of arrangement suits both you and your customers!

THE PLEASANTVILLE ROAD
LAWN BOYS

- Local Kids
- Two years of experience
- Responsible
- Reasonable prices
- Your satisfaction guaranteed!

CALL SAM AND SEAN AT 555-0879

We do it right the first time or
we do it again for free!

Rates
Mowing: $10–$30 depending on lawn size
Also available: edging, raking, and snow shovelling
Discounts available for long-term agreements

Lawn-Care Service

 My older brother Jack makes piles of money mowing lawns. Can I do this, too?

 Mowing lawns is one of the toughest jobs for kids. It takes strength and know-how. Did you know that a large lawn creates thousands of pounds of clippings in one year? If you have had lots of practice on your own grass, you might be ready to tackle other people's lawns. But, if not, you could start on a smaller scale. Ask Jack (or another mower, such as the person who cares for your church's lawn) if you could be his helper. While he mows, you can pick up sticks and twigs, trim grass around trees and walks, and rake up grass clippings. This would give you an inside view of how a successful lawn-mowing business is run. You might even take over Jack's customers when he moves on to other work!

 Other than knowing how to push a lawn mower around a yard, what do I need to know about lawn care?

 You can just do the job, or you can do the job right. Knowing these tricks of the trade will help you stand out:

- How often to mow depends on the season. Grass usually grows fastest in the spring and fall, slower in the hot summer. Change your blade height by the season. Different types of grasses have different ideal heights, but a general rule is about 1 to 2 inches (2.5 to 5 centimeters) high in cooler weather, and somewhat higher (2 to 3 inches [5 to 8 centimeters]) in warmer weather.

- Don't remove more than one third of the height at one time. Cutting too much keeps grass from manufacturing its food and exposes roots to the sun.

Smart Kids Tip

Mower Safety

Lawn mowers are powerful machines that send more than nine thousand kids to emergency rooms each year. A stone kicked out by the mower can hit someone in the eye. Fingers can be cut by rotary blades. Quite a few kids fall off riding mowers. In fact, the American Academy of Pediatrics recommends that the operation of riding mowers be limited to teens sixteen and up, and regular mowers to those twelve or older. Here are some safety tips for any lawn-care business:

- Wear hard shoes, safety goggles, earplugs, close-fitting shirts, and long pants.
- Before starting, pick up all stones and sticks and make sure young children and pets are not in the area.
- Fill the gas tank when the engine is cold.
- Turn off the engine when adjusting blade height, clearing clippings from the mower, crossing pavement, and so on.
- Don't mow a wet lawn or steep incline (you could slip).

- Keep blades sharp—get rotary blades sharpened about every eight mowings.
- Let short clippings (1 inch [2.5 centimeters] or less) filter down into the grass. You can rake up longer clippings or collect them with a bagging mower.
- If the lawn slopes, mow across rather than up and down the grade.
- Vary your mowing pattern to prevent the lawn from developing ridges.
- Keep clippings out of flowerbeds, and sweep them off walks and driveways.

Mrs. Cooper asked me to mow her lawn, but I've never even seen her backyard. How do I know what to charge?

 Walk the line. Before your mow date, ask Mrs. Cooper to take you around her property. You'll be able to estimate the amount of lawn and also find out exactly what she'd like done beyond basic mowing, such as trimming, raking clippings (and where to put them), and so on. If you still don't have a good handle on what to charge, mention that your usual rate is for average lawns that take a certain number of hours (such as $20 for about four hours). Explain that hers might cost a bit more or less.

 My friend Genna and I mow the lawns of two people on our block. What are some good ways to get more jobs?

 How about offering a sweet deal to new customers? Some examples: discount booklets (such as ten mowings for 10 percent off the usual rate), $5 off for first-time customers, discounts for seniors, a free extra service (such as weeding, trimming), and so on. Create a flyer that highlights your offer, and make sure it gets seen by lots of folks in your neighborhood. Once you reel in these new customers, your next goal is to turn them into steady jobs.

 I have lots of work during the summer, but it dries up when the grass stops growing. Any ideas?

 Turn those summer customers into year-round customers. After all, when the grass stops growing, the leaves start falling. Then the snow starts piling up, and suddenly you are back in grass-growing season again! Let your steady customers know that you are happy to handle all sorts of outdoor chores, from raking, to shoveling, to washing windows, to deadheading flowers, to clearing up storm damage. Just be sure you know how to do those jobs well before you take on clients.

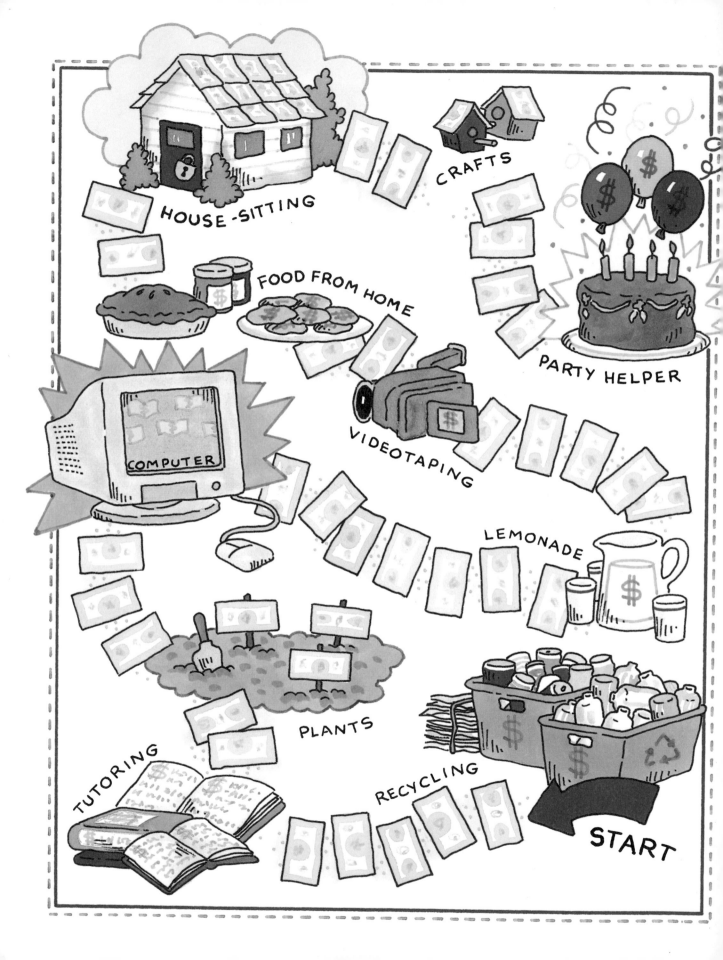

Part 3

Other Jobs

We've given fewer details on these jobs because all will vary greatly depending on where you live and what you decide to do. Many center on an interest you may already have—art, gardening, cooking, and so on.

If you can't find anyone to teach you how to turn your special talents into cash, you'll have to discover how to do it on your own. So discuss any of these jobs fully with your parents, take it slow, ask your customers lots of questions, and work out the details as you go along.

Marty's Parties

Make your child's next party the best ever!

Balloon Animals

Juggling

Jokes

Magic Tricks

$20 for a full hour of fun!
Call for a list of satisfied customers.

Marty 555-6111

Q When my cousin turned six, I helped my aunt with the party and it was really fun! Is this a good way to earn some extra money?

A One successful party won't turn you into an expert party helper, but it's a good start. Volunteer to assist at a few more kiddie parties, and soon you can use those experiences to get paying jobs.

Here are some things you might volunteer to do:

- Arrive early to help set up for the party.
- Decorate the party room.
- Prepare and serve refreshments.
- Lead sing-a-longs.

- Oversee activities—explain rules, keep kids focused on games.
- Take kids outside for an active game like tag.
- Videotape the opening of presents.
- Stay afterward to clean up.

 We have a zillion little kids in our neighborhood—someone is always having a birthday. I'd like to make money entertaining at their parties. Any ideas?

What suits your talents? Putting on a puppet show, magic performance, or juggling act? Telling mysterious or funny stories? Are you a natural clown? How about conducting a session of face painting—or a group art or cooking project? Whatever you decide to do, practice until you have a solid twenty to sixty minutes of kid-pleasing material.

Then try out your act in front of your parents and some young neighbors to fine-tune the presentation. A fun costume and a few colorful props will lend a little showbiz pizzazz to your routine.

 How do I let people know that I'm a super party assistant?

 Call your local newspaper and suggest that they stop by to watch you in action at your next assignment (after asking your customer's permission, of course). Newspapers are often interested in kids' businesses—and what photographs better than a whole roomful of laughing children? If you can't wangle some free publicity, hang flyers on the doorknobs of houses where small children live. Attaching a cute party favor will make your flyer stand out.

Garden Service

Your Garden NEEDS

The Garden Girls

We can weed,
We can plant,
We can water.

Indoor and Outdoor plants

We can help you garden or
keep your plants blooming
while you're away!

Just $10 per hour for two willing helpers
with five years of experience
in our parents' garden.

Michelle and Danielle
555-9986

 Is there some way I can make money gardening? I love plants.

 Are planting, weeding, and watering the kinds of chores you can handle easily? Then you might hire on as a helper for people with large flower or vegetable gardens. Gardeners always seem to have more tasks to do than time to do them.

Check out who in your neighborhood might need some help. Local plant nurseries and garden clubs might also be good sources for customers. But be prepared to get sweaty, dirty, and well-acquainted with lots of bugs and worms!

 I've always helped my grandfather in his garden, and now I'd like to sell my own plants. How do I get started?

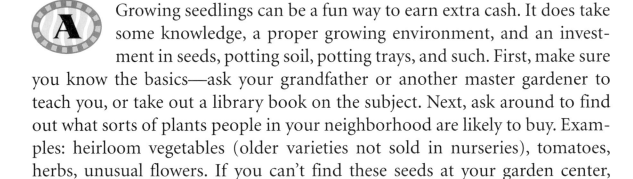 Growing seedlings can be a fun way to earn extra cash. It does take some knowledge, a proper growing environment, and an investment in seeds, potting soil, potting trays, and such. First, make sure you know the basics—ask your grandfather or another master gardener to teach you, or take out a library book on the subject. Next, ask around to find out what sorts of plants people in your neighborhood are likely to buy. Examples: heirloom vegetables (older varieties not sold in nurseries), tomatoes, herbs, unusual flowers. If you can't find these seeds at your garden center, they're available from catalogs or on the Internet.

Follow the planting instructions on the seed packet. When your seedlings have at least two sets of leaves, gently scoop them out with some surrounding soil and transplant them into individual peat pots filled with moist potting soil. Water regularly and fertilize sparingly until large enough to sell. Providing your customers with a sheet of care instructions is a nice extra touch.

Kerrie's Seedlings

Guaranteed to grow!

Reservation Form for Spring Seedlings

Customer:_____ Date of order:_____

Address:_____

Telephone:_____

Delivery deadline: ~~heil noul~~

Seedlings Reserved
($1.50 per 4-inch pot unless specified)
- Big Boy tomatoes—
- Brandywine tomatoes—
- Sweet basil—
- Lemon basil—
- Thyme—
- Catnip—
- English lavender—
- Oregano—

Kerry   655-7790

- 100% money-back guarantee on all my plants •

I make customized birdhouses

I made this one.
Do you like it?

I can make a special one for you that you'll like even more! Prices start at $15.

Jason
Please call me to view samples.
661-1129

Q Everybody (and not just my grandmother) says I'm very artistic. I like to do all kinds of crafts. Can I make some money doing that?

A Lots of people do—maybe you can, too. Can you think of a fun craft that other people (and not just your grandmother) will buy? If nothing comes to mind, look through books and magazines on crafts. You'll find instructions on how to make a variety of crafts, from birdhouses to picture frames. The Internet is also an excellent resource for ideas. So are crafts fairs. But don't jump into making products until you've asked some potential customers (neighbors or friends) if they honestly think those products will sell. Crafts take some cash and time to create, which you may never get back if you can't sell what you turn out.

 All the girls in my class are wearing hair scrunchies that cost $6 at the mall. I think I could make them for less.

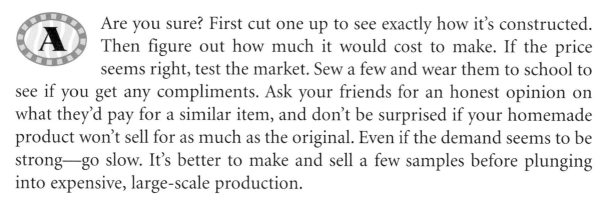 Are you sure? First cut one up to see exactly how it's constructed. Then figure out how much it would cost to make. If the price seems right, test the market. Sew a few and wear them to school to see if you get any compliments. Ask your friends for an honest opinion on what they'd pay for a similar item, and don't be surprised if your homemade product won't sell for as much as the original. Even if the demand seems to be strong—go slow. It's better to make and sell a few samples before plunging into expensive, large-scale production.

 I made a birdhouse from a book and it turned out really neat. How do I get people to buy them?

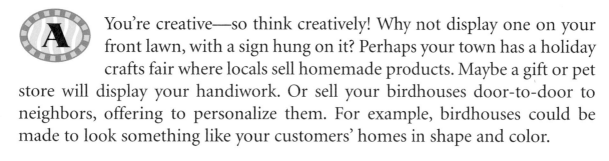 You're creative—so think creatively! Why not display one on your front lawn, with a sign hung on it? Perhaps your town has a holiday crafts fair where locals sell homemade products. Maybe a gift or pet store will display your handiwork. Or sell your birdhouses door-to-door to neighbors, offering to personalize them. For example, birdhouses could be made to look something like your customers' homes in shape and color.

Selling Foods From Home

Jams from the Johnson Family
From our own kitchen!

Thank you for buying one of our jars of cherry jam or apple butter. These products are homemade by us (Janie, Sarah, and Stephen—aged 9 to 15), with the help of our mom. We use only Empire apples and sour cherries from our grandfather's trees, which he planted in the 1960s.

The recipes come from our grandmother, Jennie Billings, who has made wonderful jams and jellies all her life (she won the blue ribbon at the Oneida County Fair in 1988). We make fewer than 50 jars of each kind a year, so we hope you enjoy the one you have purchased.

If you would like to place an order for next year, please call us at the number below. We are very proud that you chose our products!

Johnson Family Jams   **444-8885**

Q We have a big vegetable garden and there's always way too much for our family. Can I make some money selling what's left over?

A Could you set up a little veggie stand in front of your house? You might also turn your extra produce into delicious homemade foods. Some examples:

- Jams or fruit butters from berries, grapes, apples, pears, and so on
- Pickles or relishes from cucumbers, squash, red or green tomatoes
- Breads or muffins from zucchini, carrots, pumpkins

The Joy of Cooking and other basic cookbooks have recipes and detailed instructions for these and other homemade products. Food canning and preserving is a complicated process that requires adult supervision to be safe.

However, you can do many of the tasks involved—harvesting, washing, peeling, slicing, grating, stirring, applying labels, and so on. Before starting any large-scale operation, make some sample batches to fine-tune your recipes.

 For years my brother and I have made delicious strawberry jam from fruit we picked at a farm in the next county. This year we'd like to sell some of what we make. Any ideas?

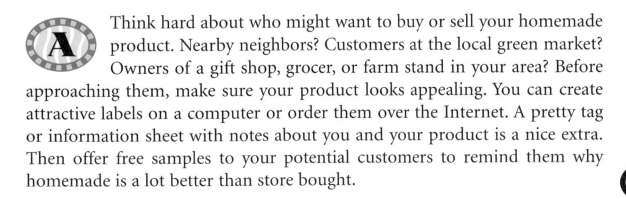 Think hard about who might want to buy or sell your homemade product. Nearby neighbors? Customers at the local green market? Owners of a gift shop, grocer, or farm stand in your area? Before approaching them, make sure your product looks appealing. You can create attractive labels on a computer or order them over the Internet. A pretty tag or information sheet with notes about you and your product is a nice extra. Then offer free samples to your potential customers to remind them why homemade is a lot better than store bought.

Computer Service

Welcome to The Computer Kid Web Site

I can make your Web site ROCK!

Contact me to find out how I can:
- Set up a site for you, your family, or your business.
- Improve your current site so it looks super!
- Teach you to make new postings to your site.
- Set up your system and introduce you to e-mail and the Internet.
- Troubleshoot your computer problems.

- Reasonable fees   •   Fast service
- Satisfaction guaranteed!

Services

Fees

Examples

About me

Contact me

Q I love working on my computer. Can I use it to make money?

A Do you have artistic or writing talent? If so, a computer can be a terrific money-making tool. Here are some ideas to explore:

- Creating holiday calendars with photos of family, house, pets
- Designing personal Web sites for families
- Creating iron-on T-shirt decals for teams, parties, families
- Producing customized greeting cards, invitations, and business cards
- Publishing a neighborhood newsletter

Some of these require special software or paper, so make sure you have a number of likely customers before spending a lot of cash on materials.

 I helped Mr. Pearson, my next-door neighbor, set up his new computer and go online. He was so grateful that he gave me a very generous tip. Can I make money helping other people with their computers?

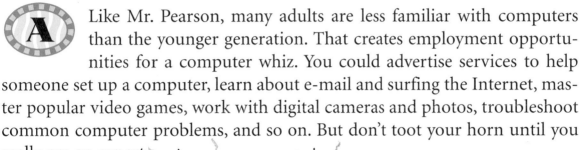 Like Mr. Pearson, many adults are less familiar with computers than the younger generation. That creates employment opportunities for a computer whiz. You could advertise services to help someone set up a computer, learn about e-mail and surfing the Internet, master popular video games, work with digital cameras and photos, troubleshoot common computer problems, and so on. But don't toot your horn until you really are an expert.

Take courses or practice at home if you need more experience in the major programs. Then consider volunteering to teach a class at a local senior center, library, or school. You'll polish your teaching skills and end up with some valuable testimonials from your pleased students—which can help you get more work.

How can I get the word out about my computer business?

You can go both hard copy (posters at local computer stores or senior centers, ads in the *Penny Saver*) and digital (your own Web site that displays examples of your work). If you have glowing testimonials from satisfied customers, use them! And since computers are an area of uncertainty for many people, consider offering a money-back guarantee. That might make people more comfortable about calling on a kid for help.

Yard-Sale Helper

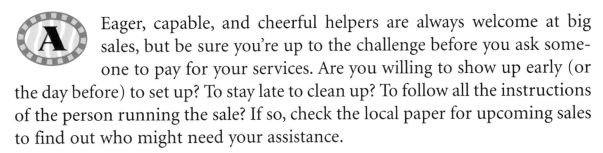

Garage and Yard Sales 2334

Are you planning a big sale?
Let us help you make it a big success! Two sisters (aged 13 and 10) with yard-sale experience can assist with setting up, displaying items attractively, selling them fast, and clearing away what's left behind. All for a very reasonable rate! Call us at 787–9980 to make your next sale the easiest and best one you've ever held!

 Shari and I had fun helping our moms with a big yard sale. Can we make money helping other families?

 Eager, capable, and cheerful helpers are always welcome at big sales, but be sure you're up to the challenge before you ask someone to pay for your services. Are you willing to show up early (or the day before) to set up? To stay late to clean up? To follow all the instructions of the person running the sale? If so, check the local paper for upcoming sales to find out who might need your assistance.

 What would make us more valuable as helpers?

 It helps to know what works best in your area. If you check out a few local sales, here are some things you might notice:

- Popular times are 8 A.M. to 2 P.M. on Friday and Saturday.
- Items are often priced between 15 percent and 30 percent of original cost, with sellers prepared to bargain.
- Things are grouped by type (such as toys) or price ($1 items only).
- Displays are at eye level or in neat boxes; prices are marked clearly.
- An extension cord is available near electric items, for testing.
- Plenty of bags are available to take home items.
- Pleasant music is playing in the background.
- Cold drinks and goodies are available for a fee, with some chairs in the shade for patient spouses.
- At multifamily sales, there are colored price labels (one color per family) that are peeled off and saved to track sales.
- Sellers have a printing calculator and lots of coins and bills for change.

 How can we help get people to come to a yard sale?

 Tell friends and neighbors, advertise in the local paper (with a list of popular items), and put up big signs like this:

> **GIANT YARD SALE**
> **14 Maple Drive**
> **8 A.M. to noon,**
> **Friday and Saturday**

Print out the words on a computer or write them with wide markers on colorful posterboard. Tack signs to the sides of large cardboard boxes, then place them at prominent corners (weighted down by putting rocks inside). A few bright balloons will help to catch people's eyes. And remember where the signs are so you can collect them once the sale is over.

Vacation House-Care Service

Go ahead—take that trip!

Leave your house and plants in the hands of the

Vacation Care Team

We are two local 6th-graders who are very responsible.
For just $2.50 a day we will:

Take in mail, packages, newspapers
Turn lights on and off
Water houseplants

You'll really enjoy your time away because you'll know

WE CARE about your house!

Call Fiona and Sue 445-0766

 Q Our neighbors go on vacation a lot. I'd like to ask them about a house-watching job, but I don't know what's involved.

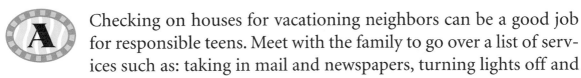 **A** Checking on houses for vacationing neighbors can be a good job for responsible teens. Meet with the family to go over a list of services such as: taking in mail and newspapers, turning lights off and on, closing and opening blinds, watering the lawn and outdoor/indoor plants, filling bird feeders, and so on. Your careful attention in this first meeting will give the owners a sense of security that their property is in good hands while they are gone.

My grandmother says checking on someone's house is a big responsibility, but it doesn't seem so hard to me. What could go wrong?

 How about killing a favorite plant by giving it too much water? Forgetting to lock the door when you leave? Setting off the alarm when you open the door? You're more likely to run into problems if you don't plan ahead, so start out by asking lots of questions. For example, have Mrs. Keene show you exactly how to get into and out of the house, and practice locking/unlocking doors and arming/disarming the house alarm while she watches. Ask Mr. Zorovich to show you exactly how to water his prize begonias, and measure how much water he uses. Use a sheet like the "Vacation Service" form on page 73 while talking to your customers.

 A house nearby was robbed last month while the owners were away. What if that happens while I'm watching the Jefferson's house?

 Safety should be your main concern—first your own and then that of the Jefferson home. Check the house during daylight rather than after dark. Does anything seem the least bit wrong when you approach or enter the house—such as an unlocked door, broken window, odd smell, or strange car in the driveway? If so, leave immediately and contact a parent or another responsible adult. Let him or her investigate or call the police or owners. The same is true for any other serious problem, such as a water leak or big branch down in the yard. Although these sorts of things very rarely happen, the owners are counting on you to act responsibly, which means telling an adult who can handle the emergency.

My Vacation Service Form

Customer's name:		

Address:		

Home phone:		

Date/time job starts:	Date/time job ends:	Payment arrangement:

EMERGENCY NUMBERS

For owner:	For neighbor:	For plumber/handyman:

House safety information (security system, fire extinguisher, flashlights, fuse box or circuit breaker, keys/locks):

Other information:

DUTIES AND INSTRUCTIONS (including when and how often)

Outdoor tasks (lawn, mail, newspaper, garden, etc.):

Indoor tasks (watering plants, lights, blinds, etc.):

Other:

Giving Lessons

 Mei Li is ten years old and lives behind us. She's way behind in reading and that's my best subject. I think I could help her. Should I ask her mother about hiring me?

 How about having a parent test the water first? Your mom or dad could find out if Mei Li's parents would be willing to pay you a small fee to work with her. If not, perhaps you'd be happy to do it for free. You'd gain some valuable experience, which might lead to paying jobs helping other kids. Other talents that could become tutoring opportunities include math, science, music, computers, and art. If no neighborhood children need your assistance, consider volunteering to tutor kids at day care or after-school programs.

Q I've been asked to help Christopher with his fourth-grade math. But I don't know where to start.

 A Talk to his parents or teacher to discover where he needs extra help. Next, become familiar with his homework to make sure you know enough to help him. Take a look at his assignment sheets, textbook, and workbook pages and do a few assignments yourself.

Once you're sure you can help, work out a tutoring schedule and decide on a goal and lesson plan for each session (ask a teacher to help you with your first one). Dream up fun ways to learn. If Christopher's problem is fractions, you might work out some hands-on activities to help him. For example, ask him to cut up a minipizza into halves and fourths and so on. Find out how he learns best—will he work longer if you take a little break every fifteen minutes? Does a contest really get him going? Maybe he'll work extra hard to get five correct answers in a row if it earns him fifteen minutes of video game playing with you when the session is done. As you go, keep notes on Christopher's progress and give his parents a report now and then.

 Q I've helped my cousins Nick and Liza improve their softball skills. How can I get more jobs like this?

 A Are you ready to volunteer as a coach's helper for after-school programs or local teams? The coaches, players, and their parents will get to know you firsthand, and you'll gain some good experience at teaching others. When the time is right, you can pass out cards or flyers about your own private coaching services (supervised by an adult, for safety's sake). If you've done a good job, adults you've worked with may be glad to act as references for you, whether your special talent is tennis, swimming, baseball, soccer, or another sport. Another paying sports job is serving as an umpire, referee, or official for local kids' games. Ask a coach how you can receive training to become the one making the calls.

Recycling Service

Willow Road Recycling Service

Too many bottles and cans and papers?
Not enough time to recycle?

We are two local boys who can help you participate fully in our town's recycling program. Call for information on how we will come to your house, pick up your items, and make the whole process easy and painless for you.

Do the right thing for just $8 per month!
Call today!

655-4367

 Our town recycling program is pretty complicated, so many of my neighbors don't participate. Can I earn some cash by helping them recycle?

 This is a job that helps your town, your neighbors, and you! To get started, become an expert on your local recycling situation. Contact local officials for full information on the rules and procedures. Find out: What materials can be recycled—newspapers, cardboard, bottles, plastics, grass clippings, leaves, metal? How are they handled—separated, washed, tied up, bagged? How are they transported—picked up by town trucks or dropped off at a center? Call your local town hall to see if there are any regulations on this sort of business. Then talk it over fully with your family to make sure they support you. You may need their help with transporting materials or setting up a recycling area in your yard, for example.

 How should I handle the recycling arrangements?

 In one town, this job might consist of working at your customer's house to sort and prepare materials for pickup. In another town, you may have to truck materials to your own house, where the recyclables are packaged before you transport them to a center. If your business is a success, consider investing in some helpful tools, such as a can crusher, newspaper bundler, or washtub for rinsing bottles.

 No one else in my town does this job. How do I know how it works?

 You don't. Since there's no business to copy when you are starting an unusual job like this one, you have to make it up as you go along. So, start small. Offer your service to two or three neighbors. Once you have worked out the best arrangements and proven your responsibility, you can add more customers.

 What's the best way to get new customers for my recycling business?

 You must convince your neighbors that recycling is a breeze, with your help. An advertising tag hung on nearby doorknobs is a good way to drum up business. New customers can be tempted with an offer of one month's service at a special low rate. When someone calls, go to the house to check out the situation and determine the most convenient arrangement.

"Convenient" is the key word here—don't expect your customers to do more than dump things into a box or garbage can. Cleaning and separating are the chores they'll be paying you to do. Since this will be a long-term arrangement (you hope), be sure to arrange for a friend or relative to be your backup if you are sick or out of town.

Magical Memories Video Service

Capture all your most precious memories on videotape forever!

8th grader with experience in taping:
- Children's Birthday Parties
- Family Reunions
- Recitals and Plays
- Award Ceremonies

Please call today to view a sample video and discuss my reasonable rates.

Craig 443-0067

Q I'm pretty good with my family's video camera. Can I make some money with this skill?

A If you are truly a video master, you might find customers among parents eager to capture the highlights of a child's birthday party, family reunion, awards ceremony, sports event, play, music recital, or even the arrival of the new puppy or baby's first haircut.

But before you go public and start selling your services, make sure you've had plenty of experience. Excuses won't cut it when the family is counting on you to memorialize little Tanya's star turn as a dancing turnip. Practice with your video camera until your skills—filming, lighting, editing, pacing—are so top notch that the final product is guaranteed to be a family treasure. And be prepared to show potential customers examples of your work.

Any tips for making a videotape really special?

 Here's some advice from the pros:

- Begin with a sign showing the occasion and date, or have someone announce it onscreen.
- If there isn't an obvious theme ("Tina Turns Ten"), then dream up one (like "10 Reasons to Love Leah" or "Charlie vs. the Cookie Monster").
- Focus on each subject for at least eight to ten seconds before moving on.
- Keep zooming to a minimum (it's distracting and drains the battery).
- Shoot from a few different angles and perspectives to add interest.
- Interview participants about what's happening ("And what happened when he opened your present?").
- For formal interviews, set up a tripod and chair in a quiet area and bring people there to talk.
- Shoot some scenes from the guests' view—walking up to the front door, greeting the host, eyeballing the decorations, zeroing in on the cake.
- Shoot children at eye level rather than from above.
- Shoot colorful elements as well as people—balloons, signs, ribbons.
- Tape family photos to mix in with the action scenes.
- To keep the sound level even, avoid facing toward loud sounds.
- Shoot outdoors if possible because light tends to be more even.
- If indoors, use the manual focus, avoid facing toward bright windows, and turn on lamps to make the lighting as even as possible.
- When filming ceremonies, recitals, or plays, bring a tripod and arrive early to find the best position and zoom settings.
- When filming pets, bring along treats and toys to get their attention.
- End with a bang—everyone waving good-bye, the star holding up a "That's All" sign, a close-up fading to black—you get the idea!

Other Jobs

TAKE A HIKE WITH MIKE!
Fun and educational nature walks in Tompkins Park for kids 7 to 12.

Mike, Eagle Scout
992-6013

Hate to do windows?
Call me for fast and excellent service, indoor and outdoor.
Roger 444–6312

Cooking with Carol!
Cooking lessons for kids
Your kitchen or mine
Carol 311–8488
A great birthday party idea!

The Bike Boys
We'll keep your bike in top shape! Tuneups, maintenance, minor repairs.

Kevin and Jaleel
656-8885

Q The usual kids' jobs don't really appeal to me. What other jobs are there?

A What do adults not want to do—and will pay **you** to do instead? This can range from cleaning out an overflowing garage to entertaining cranky kids for an hour. Once you have an idea, you can create informational business cards by using special paper and a computer graphics program. Following are some ideas to get you started on dreaming up that dream job:

- Astronomy guide—host nightly sessions with your telescope
- Bike tune-ups—do minor repairs on bikes and scooters
- Compost service—establish a compost pile and sell compost to gardeners
- Dance teacher—teach folk dancing or the latest dance craze
- Decoration service—put up and take down lights, streamers, and such for parties or holidays
- Flower stand—sell flowers from your garden, make dried-flower wreaths or arrangements
- Gift service—do creative wrappings and cards
- Holiday event service—organize Easter-egg hunts, pumpkin-carving contests, and other fun events
- Show organizer—put on a play, quiz show, bike race, or puppet show for the neighborhood
- Sign-language teacher—instruct those who want to learn
- Singer—form a group to sing at events, lead kids in sing-alongs at parties
- Storyteller—read books or tell stories to kids at your house or theirs

Mainly for older kids:

- Errand service—mail packages, return videos, pick up dry cleaning, shop for groceries, and so on
- Home helper—clean out and organize garages, attics, playrooms; sweep sidewalks and porches; wash windows; keep birdfeeders filled and cleaned; clean pools; shine shoes
- Lunch delivery—cater to businesspeople who can't leave their workplaces
- Moving helper—packing, unpacking, cleaning up
- Nature guide—take kids on nature walks and teach them about local plants, insects, etc.
- Outdoor painting—furniture, fences, doghouses, decks, storage sheds, window boxes

Part 4

Tips for Success

Lots of kids start a new job with great enthusiasm—and then give it up when it turns out to be not quite as easy and profitable as expected. This chapter is designed to help you avoid some common frustrations (such as too few customers, too little money) and make your work experience as successful as possible.

Thinking About
Money

 Q Last Saturday we sold all our lemonade at twenty-five cents a cup and we were really happy—until we added everything up. We lost money! How did that happen?

 A It's easy to lose track of your finances when you start a business. But put your math skills to work and take a look at what happened on Saturday:

- You earned $12.50 by selling 50 cups of lemonade at 25¢ each (50 x 25¢ = $12.50)
- But you spent $18.29—$5.79 more than you earned ($18.29 − $12.50 = $5.79)

Bummer! To get a handle on how that happened, you need to understand the many expenses involved in doing business.

 Q What are business expenses?

 A There are two basic types—supply and overhead expenses:

Supply Expenses
These are the things that you use up as you do business. Following is your total per-cup expense:

Lemonade	$5.34	(6 cans for 89¢ each, enough for 50 cups of lemonade)
Straws	.70	(for package of 50)
Cups	3.00	(for package of 50)
Napkins	.75	(for package of 50)
Ice	1.30	(for large bag)
Total	**$11.09**	**(divided by 50 cups = 22¢ per cup)**

Overhead Expenses

These are items you buy just once but use again. These costs are spread over the total time the items are used. Here are your total overhead expenses:

Oak-tag signs	$1.20
Tablecloth	2.50
Balloons	1.00
Big marker	2.50
Total	**$7.20** **(divided by 50 cups = 15¢ per cup)**

Your total per-cup expense is:

Supply expense	$11.09	(22¢ per cup)
Overhead expense	7.20	(15¢ per cup)
Total expense	**$18.29**	**(37¢ per cup)**

Now deduct your sales price from your total expense to see what your profit or loss is:

Total expense	$18.29
Sales price	- 12.50
Loss	**- 5.79 (you lost 12¢ per cup)**

According to these figures, you'd have to charge 12¢ more per cup—just to break even.

What can we do to be sure we make money rather than lose it?

 There are three ways to make a profit more likely: (1) You can spread your overhead costs over a number of days (sell for six days rather than one), (2) you can raise your price, or (3) you can cut down on expenses. Here's what happens if you do all three for this stand:

- Spreading overhead costs (signs, balloons) over 6 days saves $1.20 a day. ($7.20 ÷ 6 = $1.20)

- Charging 10¢ more per cup brings in $5.00 more a day. (50 x 10¢ = $5.00)

- Borrowing (rather than buying) a marker and tablecloth saves 83¢ a day. ($2.50 + $2.50 ÷ 6 = 83¢)

- Making your own ice saves $1.30 a day while not buying straws saves 70¢ a day.

- Buying a bigger and cheaper package of napkins saves 20¢ a day. ($3.30 for a large package divided by 6 = 55¢ a day)

- Buying reusable cups (and washing them) saves you $1.75 a day.

If you do all this, here's how the money shakes out:

Supplies for 1 day	$ 7.50	(15¢ per cup x 50)
Overhead for 1 day	.50	(1¢ per cup x 50)
Total expenses	**$8.00**	(16¢ per cup x 50)
Total sales	**$17.50**	(35¢ per cup x 50)
Profit	**$ 9.50**	(19¢ per cup x 50)

Profit and loss can be even more complicated than this. (You might sell fewer cups of lemonade on some days, for instance.) But it's worthwhile to consider all the hidden costs involved in your business. Then you can set a price that gives you a reasonable profit.

Check out the "My Business Plan" form at the back of this book to see how the numbers might crunch for your own business.

Thinking About
What to Charge

 Q My brother and I mow lawns in our neighborhood and everybody pays us a different amount.

 A Picture this: You're shopping for video games, but there are no prices on them. You pick one out and hand the clerk $7.85, which is what you decide it's worth to you. Does this make sense?

Obviously, a store can't work this way—and neither should your business. It's standard practice for the price of a product or service to be fixed up front, so that both the buyer and seller know exactly what's involved when a purchase is made.

That said, a study shows that most kids don't discuss payment before they take on a job—they let the customer decide what to pay them. Sure, you may get lucky now and then with a generous client, but the businesslike approach is to agree on a fair price before you begin the work.

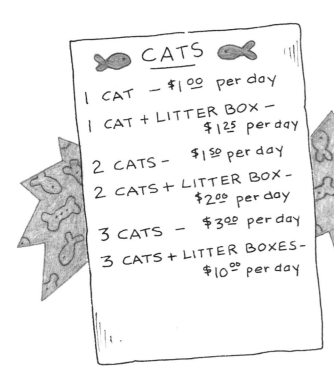

CATS
- 1 CAT — $1.00 per day
- 1 CAT + LITTER BOX — $1.25 per day
- 2 CATS — $1.50 per day
- 2 CATS + LITTER BOX — $2.00 per day
- 3 CATS — $3.00 per day
- 3 CATS + LITTER BOXES — $10.00 per day

DOGS
- 1 DOG - WALK + FEED — $2.50 per day
- 1 DOG OVER 50 LBS — $3.50 per day
- 1 DOG WHO HIDES UNDER SOFA — $1.50 per day
- 1 DOG WHO GROWLS — $5.00 per day
- 1 EXCITABLE DOG — $8.00 per day

How can I know the fair price?

 There are two main ways to set a fee:

- Find out what other kids in your neighborhood are charging for the same sort of work. Your parents and neighbors can help you find out what other kids generally charge for a small, medium, or large lawn, for example.

- Determine what amount is a fair payment to cover your expenses plus the time you put in. Some kids' businesses (like baby-sitting and pet care) have few or no expenses, but others have costs like gasoline.

  Adults often expect a bargain when hiring a kid, so the minimum wage (usually under $6 an hour) can be a useful starting point when figuring payment for your time. That amount is often paid to teenagers with job experience. The younger or less experienced you are, the less you'd be expected to charge for the hours you put in on the task. The ease or difficulty of the work can also affect the fee. For example, you could probably charge more per hour for digging up stumps than watering a garden. Also consider whether this is a one-time or steady job—steady customers always appreciate a discount of some sort.

 Do I need to draw up a contract?

 Most kids' jobs are handled without a written contract (a signed statement that describes the job and payment). However, sometimes a simple version can nail down expectations for you and your customer. Following are two examples:

Contract A:
- Carrie Pepper will deliver 10 healthy tomato seedlings (5 Big Boy and 5 Roma Beauty) in 6-inch pots to Mrs. Tholls on May 31.

- If they are acceptable, Mrs. Tholls will pay Carrie $2.00 per seedling.
- Signed: Jane Tholls, Carrie Pepper, March 15.

Contract B:

- Henry Leung will create a Web site for the Utrecht family. It will consist of three pages: Home Page, What's New, Contact Us. Pages will have text and photos provided by the family, plus clipart illustrations.

- Family will deliver text and photos to Henry by June 15. Henry will create a first draft by July 1. He will make requested changes by July 15. He will launch the site on the Internet once it is finally approved. Planned date for the launch is July 20.

- Henry will be paid $6.50 an hour for his work, with a job estimate of 10 to 15 hours ($65–$100). He will keep a careful accounting of his time. If it begins to look like it will go over that amount, Henry will inform Mr. Utrecht before continuing.

- Henry has received $20 in advance, to be deducted from the final cost of this job. If for any reason the Utrecht family decides to cancel this job before June 15, Henry will return the deposit.

- Signed on May 15 by: Henry Leung, John Utrecht.

Thinking About
Getting Customers

 My brother David and I have a magic show we'd like to do for birthday parties. It's really good and our little cousins loved it. But that's the only job we've gotten so far. How can we get more customers?

 How much time have you two spent perfecting your magic show? Two days, two weeks, even longer? Many businesspeople spend as much time and effort promoting their businesses (working to get new customers) as doing the work itself. That's a fact!

It's rare for a job to walk up and knock on your door—usually you have to go out and hunt it down. As you read about the jobs for kids in this book, pay attention to the ways to make customers aware that you're ready and willing to work for them.

 What are some advertising methods we could use?

 Here are some good ways to get more customers:

- Ask your customers, neighbors, and family for "referrals" (friends who might be interested in hiring you) and contact everyone they suggest.
- Pin up signs (with tear-off phone numbers) at the post office, supermarkets, community bulletin boards, and so on.
- Place an inexpensive ad in a community paper (such as the *Penny Saver*).
- Hang your ads on the front doorknobs around your neighborhood.
- Put out a big sign giving your business name and phone number when you are doing an outdoor job.
- Create a Web site for your business.

- Send holiday cards to people who might become customers.
- Wear a T-shirt printed with your business and phone number.
- Suggest to the local newspaper that you and your business would make a good article.
- Send a newsletter about your business to current and potential customers.
- If you make a product, give out free samples with your business name and number attached.
- Offer a bargain rate to attract new customers.

Many promising businesses fail because they just don't spend enough time and effort on advertising. Don't let that happen to you!

Thinking About Working for Adults

 Q How do I get adults to hire me? I want to start washing cars on my block, but I'm a little shy about asking my neighbors.

 A Some kids have no problem talking to adults. Others need a little practice. After all, asking for work isn't the same as chatting in the kitchen with your best friend's mom.

First impressions are very important, so before approaching neighbors about washing their cars, make sure you look neat and clean. Wearing your rattiest T-shirt and jeans will not impress anyone. Also, think about what you're going to say.

Since you have just one shot at making a good first impression, you might practice first in front of your parents. Brainstorm questions a customer might ask, then put those facts into your presentation or prepare good responses. Work up a two-minute speech describing your qualifications and fees. If you have a flyer to hand out, you can focus on drawing attention to the points you've made there.

 Q Do I have to ask about work in person?

 A Some kids find it easier to make a first contact over the phone (it helps to practice that speech ahead of time, too) or to slip a flyer under the door. Eventually you'll have to talk face-to-face, but sometimes that's easier once the ice is broken.

Whether it's dealing with Mr. Singh about washing his car or Mrs. Keebler about baby-sitting, adults appreciate politeness. Asking if this is a convenient time to talk (and thanking them for their time) can make a big difference.

Thinking About
References

Mrs. Simonson asked me about setting up her new computer, then asked for my references. I'm not sure what references are— so how do I get some?

A reference is a report on your good work, usually from a customer. Because people like to be told by another adult that a young person can handle a job, good references will boost your chances of getting work.

Sometimes a reference is written down, so you can copy it and pass it along to Mrs. Simonson or others. But often you'll simply provide the name and phone number of your reference, so he or she can be called to discuss your qualifications.

Do you have a satisfied customer who can vouch for your responsibility and skill at this job? If so, the first step is to ask permission to use him or her as a reference. Try to make this very easy to do, such as using e-mail to request a written reference. Your customer can shoot back a "reply" statement with no bother at all.

When it comes to telephone references, be careful about "using them up." A reference who is called again and again will live to regret the decision to help you. Tell possible customers that you can provide references "on request," but don't hand out the contact information to anyone who isn't really serious about hiring you.

What if I'm new at a job and don't have any happy customers yet?

References can come from anyone who has witnessed your good work habits. Think about asking your teacher, clergyman, coach, scout leader, or another adult if they would be willing to vouch for you.

Still come up short? Maybe it's time to go out and get some real experience. Consider volunteering for a local program and then asking the adult in charge to be a reference for you.

 Should I use references in my advertising?

 You can get a lot of mileage out of your references by quoting them (omitting the names, of course, for privacy's sake) in your advertising. For example:

"Geoff had my computer up and running in just 15 minutes!"
—Juniper Street resident

"I don't worry about taking a trip now that Terri is my pet-sitter. My cats love to see her come."
—Handsome Hal and Fluffy's owner

"Sheryl is one of the most responsible students in my science class."
—7th-grade teacher at Harrison Middle School

Thinking About
Competition

Mrs. Fernandez just moved in next door. There are two kids who mow lawns on my road—me and Chuck. I'd really like this job, so what should I do?

Try to get to Mrs. Fernandez first with your pitch—that often gives you an inside edge on a job. The simplest way is to talk to her directly. You could catch her in the yard or call for an appointment. If you're too shy for a direct approach, create a flyer listing your qualifications and slip it under her door.

I've been pet-sitting in my neighborhood for nearly six months, but lately another girl, Jill, seems to get more jobs than I do. What should I do?

Uh-oh. Looks like you've got some tough competition. Welcome to the world of work—to be successful at a popular job like lawn care or pet-sitting, sometimes you need to check out your competition. What is Jill doing to make her customers happy? How much is she charging? Ask your parents for help if you can't dig up these facts on your own. The next step is to think about what you could do to offer people a better deal than Jill provides. Maybe you could charge a little less or offer additional services, like poop scooping or cleaning out litter boxes. Also think about the kind of job you've been doing for people. Have you been following their instructions and showing up on time? Have you been friendly and polite?

Whether they want to mow lawns or wash cars, baby-sit or walk dogs, smart kids check out their competition and concentrate on building an excellent reputation.

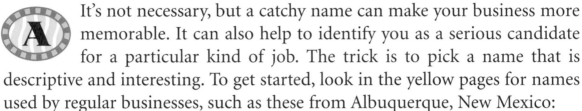

Thinking About
Naming Your Business

Do I have to have a name for my business?

It's not necessary, but a catchy name can make your business more memorable. It can also help to identify you as a serious candidate for a particular kind of job. The trick is to pick a name that is descriptive and interesting. To get started, look in the yellow pages for names used by regular businesses, such as these from Albuquerque, New Mexico:

Smiling Faces Child Care

TruGreen Land Care

Barbara's Pet Parade

Mac Happy Computer Services

Any tips for creating a good name?

Why not have some fun when choosing a name? Here are some tips to get you started:

- Use your name, location, or description of your business.

    Jenny's Beautiful Button Jewelry
    Terry's Tasty Tomatoes
    The Third Avenue Car Wash Team
    The Recycling Boys
    Kids Who Kare for Kats (and Dogs)

- Tack on a descriptive phrase to highlight what makes you special.

    The Garage Sale Angels—We'll help make your next sale a success!
    Josh's Tutoring—Making math and science fun!
    Sean's Computer Services—Get friendly with your PC

Loren's Party Video Service—Memories for a lifetime
Pet Care by Karen—Loving your pet when you're not home
Snow Be Gone!—Never shovel your walk again
Terrific T-Shirts—Make your team stand out
Leaf Busters—Got dead leaves? Who you gonna call?
Homemade Jam by the Harris Sisters—Fresh from our backyard

 Is a logo a good idea?

You might try designing your own logo (a special graphic of the business name) if you have a graphics program on your computer. Experiment with different kinds of type and maybe even an illustration. When you have something you like, print copies in both black and white and color, if possible. Your logo can be resized on a copy machine if you want to use it on your advertising materials.

Thinking About
Your Parents and Your Job

 I'm starting to mow lawns for a few of my neighbors and now my parents want to know all about what I'm doing. Shouldn't they butt out?

 No. Your parents are, of course, concerned with everything that might affect your health or safety. And they are also legally responsible for any mistakes you might make. No wonder they want to know exactly what's up!

In many cases, your business won't fly without some assistance from your mom or dad. Here are just a few of the ways your parents can help you:

- Provide advice (on business name, publicity ideas, good locations, ways to deal with adults, and so on)
- Lend or give you money or materials to get started
- Help you deal with your finances (estimate costs, decide on fees, get a bank account)
- Provide transportation to your customers or to stores for supplies
- Help you check out a work situation before you start
- Assist you in finding customers (asking friends, calling neighbors)
- Handle emergencies when things go wrong

The earlier you include them in your planning, the better. After all, you'll need their sign-off on whether you're old enough to baby-sit or handle a riding mower, skilled enough to make jam, responsible enough to take care of pets, and so on.

How do I get the job discussion started?

Why not use the "My Job Plan" form at the end of this book? Pencil in your own ideas, then sit down with your parents to fully discuss them. Suppose they're not quite as sure as you are that you're ready for a big leap into the world of work. Jump at the opportunity to show them how mature you can be. Draw up a list of their objections and your responses, like this:

Objection A: The job will take time away from your homework.

Response: I promise to always get my homework done before I go to the job. If I can't manage this, I will quit the job.

Objection B: You don't know how to do this job right.

Response: I will ask my customer exactly what she wants done, and write down what she says. After I have done the job a few times, I will ask if there is any way I can improve my performance.

Face it. You are much more likely to succeed if you have your family solidly behind you. So take all the time necessary to work out the details with them before you set off on your big money-making adventure.

Thinking About

Standing Out

 Q Other kids around here have been baby-sitting longer than I have. Why would someone hire me?

 A Ask yourself two questions.

First, what is your *experience* with this type of work? Count your life experience, not just paying jobs. For example, have you taken care of younger brothers or sisters, babies, toddlers, twins, disabled kids, and so on? If you want to be a garden helper, how many people have you assisted in their gardens; what plants have you raised? A garage-sale helper could add up all the days helping with any group sales activity—bake sales, church fairs, charity car washes, cookie sales, and so on.

Second, what special *qualifications* do you have? Maybe you can capture any child's attention with a story or can tutor a third-grader in math. A dog walker might have a strong ball-throwing arm (good for giving a retriever a really good workout). A computer whiz might have won an award for designing a school club Web site.

 Q I really don't have much in the way of experience or qualifications. Now what?

 A Go out and get some. That's not as hard as it sounds. Is it baby-sitting you are interested in? Here are some things you can do to stand out (with examples on what a sitter might do in each case).

- Volunteer at a well-known place (help out at a church day-care program).
- Take a course (first aid, child development, baby-sitting basics).
- Develop a skill (learn how to tutor children in reading or math).
- Offer yourself as a backup (to other sitters in your area).

- Offer a special service (put together a "fun kit" you can bring along).
- Gather references (from the adults for whom you've worked).

Once you have something to crow about, go right ahead and crow! Ask your current customers for the names of friends who might be interested in your services. Then send them a flyer that highlights all your special qualities. Add quotes from your glowing references. After all, how will potential customers know how terrific you are if you don't tell them?

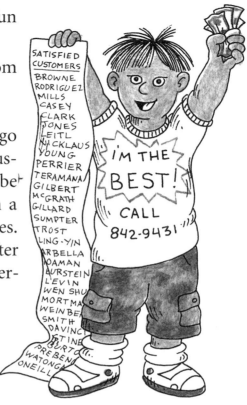

Thinking About
Following Up With Customers

 I took care of Mrs. Reilly's cat, Sooty, for a week, but she hasn't asked me to pet-sit again. Did I do something wrong?

You'll never know if you don't ask. Customers do like to be thanked for their business and asked if they were totally satisfied. If it hasn't been too long since the job (under two weeks), feel free to pick up the phone and do just that. Tell her you're eager to do a good job and honestly want to learn from any mistakes you might have made.

Hopefully, you'll hear that she was very pleased and expects to hire you again. But if she brings up any concerns or problems, listen very carefully. Maybe you forgot to lock the back door or clean the litter box thoroughly. Try to turn any bad experience into a good one. Volunteer to care for Sooty again for free. That's an offer she might not be able to refuse, and a first step in turning Mrs. Reilly into a repeat customer for a long time to come.

What if too much time has passed for that?

 How about sending a "Thanks for Your Business" note or card? You could include one or more of these items:

- A money-back guarantee, promising full satisfaction
- 20 percent off the next two jobs
- Booklet with five $1 coupons
- Short survey form asking for a satisfaction rating and comments, with a $2 off discount coupon for mailing it back

For all new or major jobs, make it a part of your routine to call or write each customer to let them know how much you appreciate their business. Thank Mr. Sampson for choosing you to wash his cars. Let Mrs. Goff know that she can sign up for a weekly weeding service and get $1 off each session. Tell Mrs. Ewell that you'd be pleased to mow her yard again for free if your first cut didn't meet her standards.

Saying thank you (and meaning it) isn't just being polite. It's good business.

Thinking About Problem Solving

 What do you do when everything goes wrong? First I broke the water dish. Then Muffin piddled on the white rug. I'm afraid the Andrews will be really mad when they get home.

 Yes, bad things happen now and then. A broken dish, a door left unlocked, a misunderstanding on the baby-sitting date. Rule #1: Don't even try to cover up the problem. That only proves for sure that you can't be trusted. The Andrews do realize that even adults can make mistakes and that you're not an adult. Honesty is always the best policy when dealing with your customers.

In this case, leave a note with an apology and an offer to repair or replace the dish. Muffin's little accident probably wasn't your fault, but you should mention it and ask how they'd like you to handle that sort of thing in the future. Your goal is to act like a responsible person who can be trusted to make good decisions.

 Any tips for preventing problems?

 Can you stop problems before they pop up? Often you can—by sitting down with family members or friends who've done similar jobs and talking about what might go wrong. Ask, "What are the worst things that could happen?" Then think up solutions. A cat-sitter might come up with a list like this:

Problem—cat seems afraid of me

Make friends with cat ahead of time, bring treats, play games with cat.

Problem—cat might have "accidents" inside house

Have products on hand to clean up messes, keep cat's litter box clean.

Problem—cat could get sick

Ask owner about cat's health, get phone numbers for vet and where owner can be reached.

Problem—cat could run away

Make sure all doors are locked, be careful when going in and out of the house.

Problem—you might forget dates of the job

Write dates down on calendar, call to confirm dates before the job starts, check before stopping the job to make sure owner has returned.

Problem—you might be too sick to care for the cat

Ask reliable friend to be a backup sitter.

Problem—you might lose the house key

Keep key on a string around neck, ask owner to leave extra key with neighbor.

Problem—something might look wrong when entering the house

You know that you should never enter a house if something looks wrong. Instead you've worked out a contingency plan with your parents. You go to your parents or a trusted adult for help, and you always have these numbers at hand: police, fire department, friend of owner, owner's emergency number.

Part 5

Your Job Plan

Ready to tackle the world of work? Not so fast! First, sit down with the "My Job Plan" form and answer all twelve questions about the particular job you have in mind. Go over the details carefully with your family and partner (if you have one). You're much more likely to be successful if you catch most of your mistakes on paper rather than on the job!

My Job Plan

Use this form to think out and then write down your ideas about a job. Then discuss these plans with your family and partner(s) to work out the details.

1. My name:
2. What kind of job would I like to do?
3. What are the products and/or services?
4. Who can give me advice about this job?
5. Should I have a partner? Who? What will each of us do?
6. Who will be my customers?
7. What research should I do ahead of time?
8. What supplies and equipment will I need? How much will they cost?
9. How much should I charge?
10. What can I do to get customers?
11. What references from adults do I have?
12. What else do I need to think about before I start this job?

For More Information

Here are some useful Web sites that were current when this book went to press. And new ones are popping up all the time! Just use any search engine to look for them.

For information on pets
www.cherishedmoments.com/safety-tips-for-kids-petlovers.htm
www.walking-a-dog.com
www.bathing-a-dog.com
www.catsinternational.org
www.spca.org

On car washing
ok.essortment.com/carwashingtip=rvjj.htm/

On baby-sitting
www.urbanext.uiuc.edu/babysitting
www.redcross.org/services/hss/courses/tips.html
www.kidshealth.org—search for babysitting
www.funology.com

On lawn mowing
www.doityourself.com/lawn/lawnmowingmadeeasy.htm
www.lawn-tips.com

On lemonade stands
www.coolmath4kids.com/lemonade/
sunkist.com/kids/lemonadestand.asp

For other information on kids and jobs
www.family.go.com/raisingkids/learn/activities/feature/famf0600sumjob/
www.kidsmoney.org
www.raw-connections.com/garden/index.htm—*gardening*
www.craftsfortrade.com—*craft ideas*
www.foodsafety.gov—*click on consumer advice*
www.yardsalequeen.com—*yard sales*
www.frugalfamily.com/finance/SellingTips.asp—*yard sales*
sfsv.org/tutor.html—*tutoring*
alephnull.net/eco—*recycling*
www.camcorderinfo.com/info/goodvideo.htm—*videotaping*